welcome

You want to knit but you don't know how. You're not alone! Even though it seems like everyone is knitting, many crafters are in your situation, yearning for the joy, creativity, and calm that knitting brings.

If you've decided you're ready to learn to knit, take the time to practice each of the skills as they are presented in this publication. Don't move to the next skill until you've mastered the one you're working on. Finding a knitter to coach you will speed things along. It won't be more than a few days before you'll be able to start your first project.

In *1-2-3 knit* we present all the knitting techniques you'll need to make all the projects in the issue (plus lots of others). The basic English method for knitting—the standard for the United States—is the one we teach. You may know people that knit using the Continental method (knitting with the yarn in their left hand and "picking" the yarn with the needle from their right hand). This is a great technique to learn as well, but since space is limited, we are offering the most common method. Both methods are equally fast—with practice! So, grab some knitting needles and yarn, turn to page 4, and learn to knit!

Then when you're ready to advance from working practice swatches to making a project, look at our terrific collection beginning on page 32. All of the designs are easy to knit—the bright variegated place mats on page 42 and the "mile"-long scarf on page 38 are excellent, quick-to-finish beginner choices. As you get more confident and adventuresome, try one of the afghans on pages 46 and 48 or the classic "first" pullover on page 62.

Most of all, have fun learning a skill you'll enjoy for a lifetime!

The Staff

table of **contents**

19

knitting basics

knitting projects

38

42

50

getting the
knitting urge

These days, it seems everyone is knitting or learning to knit. What's all the "knit 1, purl 1" buzz about?

PHOTOGRAPHER: PERRY STRUSE

Are you getting caught up in all the knitting excitement? Drop by your local yarn shop, and you'll truly be smitten!

Even if you haven't yet learned the technique, it's worth a visit to a yarn shop just to be inspired. There, you'll discover shelves stacked with the latest yarns from the world over. Colors from brights to pastels—sometimes combined in a single yarn—will dazzle you. The textures are endless, too: soft, thick-and-thin, crisp, silky-smooth, furlike, and nubby.

And if the yarn isn't enough to get you rallied 'round a pair of knitting needles, check out the patterns. They're spectacular! Today's knitting designers are prolific, providing abundant projects for all skill levels. Look to books and publications like this one for striking hand-knit garments and fashion accessories as well as for handsome accents for your home decor.

Never fear—help is here.

When you pay a visit to your local yarn shop, feel free to ask for help—today, tomorrow, and all throughout your knitting adventures. More than likely, the shop owner and the assistants are experienced knitters. In addition to helping you with your purchases, they should be able to assist you with any reasonable requests you have regarding a particular knitting project or problem.

Many independent shops—and some large retailers—offer classes on topics ranging from simple basics to intarsia knitting. You may want to take advantage of one or more of these, too.

So grab your needles!

Filled with great-looking projects compiled especially for beginners, this booklet serves as a handy reference tool to help you learn and/or refresh your knowledge of the basic stitches and knitting techniques.

The knitting outlook is explosive! Get hooked, and you'll fill your days (and spare moments) with beautiful yarns, projects, and the relaxing "k 1, p1" clicks of the needles as you knit away.

knittingbasics

knit one, purl one

Sounds easy enough—and it is! This section covers the basics: from learning about the supplies, abbreviations, and stitches to discovering techniques for making each project perfect.

choosing yarn

Selecting the yarn for your project involves more than simply picking out the prettiest color.

PHOTOGRAPHER: DEAN TANNER

You've chosen your pattern and plan to make it just as it appears in the photograph. No problem. But what happens when you get to the yarn store and see all those fabulous yarns? You just might be tempted to make a change! The information that follows will help you become more knowledgeable about yarns and will assist you when making yarn substitutions and selections.

Natural, synthetic, or blend? When choosing a fiber, think about the end use of your project. Natural fibers such as wool, mohair, alpaca, cotton, cashmere, and linen are excellent for adult garments. Synthetics (acrylic, nylon, and blended fibers) are better selections for items such as place mats or children's clothing—the kinds of items that require repeated washing. Novelty yarns and ribbons also are available. If you decide on the yarn before you select your knitted pattern, be sure to ask a salesperson to help you find a design that's appropriate for your yarn and your skill level.

In discussions about yarns, you'll often hear knitters mention weight. This has nothing to do with ounces or pounds. Weight refers to bulkiness—how thick or thin a yarn strand is. Yarns are classified by weight as super fine, fine, light, medium, bulky, and super bulky. Yarns for baby layettes, for example, usually fall under the fine and light weight categories; yarns for men's sweaters are more likely to fall under medium and bulky weight.

Your yarn selection affects the needle size you'll need to use for your project. Generally speaking, a range of three needle sizes is appropriate for knitting the yarns in each of the categories. Refer to the chart on the next page for the categories, types of yarn by weight within the categories, and recommended needle sizes.

Yarn labels will identify yarns and usually recommend needle sizes. Increasing numbers of companies are identifying their yarns, utilizing a universal system adopted by the Yarn Council of America that makes it easier

For information on knitting standards and more, go to www.yarnstandards.com.

yarn weight chart

yarn categories	super fine	fine	light	medium	bulky	super bulky
	1	**2**	**3**	**4**	**5**	**6**
yarn types	sock, fingering, baby	sport, baby	dk*, light worsted	worsted, afghan, aran	chunky, craft, rug	bulky, roving
gauge for 4 inches in stockinette stitch	27–32 sts	23–26 sts	21–24 sts	16–20 sts	12–15 sts	6–11 sts
recommended needle sizes in metric	2.25–3.25 mm	3.25–3.75 mm	3.75–4.5 mm	4.5–5.5 mm	5.5–8 mm	8 mm & larger
recommended needle sizes in U.S. sizes	1–3	3–5	5–7	7–9	9–11	11 & larger

*double-knitting

to choose yarns and patterns that work well together. Look for the weight number on the label that's printed on the universal logo: **1**

On the label you'll also find fiber content, care instructions, gauge and needle size recommendations, the amount (in yards and/or meters), package weight (in ounces and/or grams), dye lot, and color number. Keep the labels until you finish your project. This will make it easier to purchase more of the same—or suitably similar—color and dye lot should you run out of yarn.

It's also a good idea to buy an extra ball of yarn when you're making your initial purchase in case of an unforeseen problem. Provided the yarn hasn't been unwrapped and you've saved the receipt, you should be able to return it to your yarn shop for a refund or credit. Be sure to ask about the shop's policy.

Overwhelmed? Don't be. This all will become second nature to you as you become increasingly comfortable with the craft. Soon you may find the only difficult decision is choosing which project to start on first!

yarn weights *shown actual size*

super fine

fine

light

medium

bulky

super bulky

outfit your
knitting bag

Once you begin knitting a project, you'll need a way to keep your supplies organized and at hand. Check out these suggestions.

PHOTOGRAPHER: DEAN TANNER

The best way to make progress on your knitting is to take it with you—everywhere you go—in a handy, generous-size knitting bag. If you're like many knitters and you have several projects going at once, it's a good idea to keep an assortment of bags on hand. They can be anything from sturdy plastic sacks to canvas totes or carryalls created especially for knitters.

Many knitters have discovered that if they prepare a small kit filled with the basic knitting accessories, they can quickly move it from one project bag to the next. Choose a fabric or plastic cosmetics container (one of the free ones you get with another purchase is perfect), or buy a smaller knitting bag to hold all your supplies. The items identified at right and shown *opposite* are helpful tools for almost any project you want to knit, and they should easily fit into your kit.

tools of the trade

A Flexible Straight Needles
B Knitting Needle Point Protectors
C Circular Needle
D Double-Pointed Needles (dpns)
E Thread Cutter Pendant
F Tape Measure
G Crochet Hook (for picking up dropped stitches)
H Blunt-End Yarn Needles
I Cable Needle
J Row Counters (two styles shown)
K Stitch Marker Rings
L Split-Ring Markers
M Spool Knitter and Needle (for trims)
N Stitch Holder
O Stitch-Gauge Tool

needle notes

Standard, double-pointed, or circular? Knitting has many needle styles. How do you know which kind to use?

PHOTOGRAPHER: DEAN TANNER

Knitting needles come in assorted shapes and sizes, and they're made from a variety of materials. How do you choose the right ones? Once you select your yarn and pattern, it will be easy to determine the needles best suited to your project.

Standard knitting needles (the ones you're most familiar with) come in pairs and usually in lengths of 10 and 14

inches. Tapered at one end, they're protected with a "stop" at the other to prevent stitches from slipping off the back end. These needles are used to work a sizable number of knitting stitches (depending upon the bulkiness of the yarn) and are designed so you can knit back and forth in rows. They can be made of plastic, metal, bamboo, or other woods, including even fine hardwoods such as rosewood and birch.

Double-pointed needles (dpns) are designed for projects knitted in rounds. Available in plastic, metal, and wood, they come in sets of four or five and usually in lengths of 7 and 10 inches. The needles are tapered at both ends and are used to knit items such as caps, socks, mittens, and sweater sleeves. They are used in pairs for knitting I-cords, and you also might use two of them at once for row-knitting narrow pieces, such as a purse strap, when it's easier to work on a short needle. When row-knitting, wrap a rubber band around the back end of each needle to prevent the knitted stitches from slipping off.

Circular needles can be used for both circular and row knitting. A nylon cord connects the two needles, creating one long needle tapered at both ends. Made of the same materials used in double-pointed needles, they're available in 16-, 24-, 26-, 28-, 32-, and 36-inch lengths. The two shorter

lengths (16- and 24-inch) work well for making caps and sweaters. The longer needles hold many more stitches and make it easier to knit shawls or afghans.

The size designation of a needle is not a reference to its length but to its widest diameter. Both U.S. and metric systems identify these sizes. For the U.S. system, needles run in a numbered series from 1 to 50, with 1 as the smallest. Metric sizes represent the actual metric measurements, from 2.25 millimeters to 25 millimeters.

The chart below shows metric and U.S. sizes.

Knitting Needle Sizes

Metric Range	U.S. Size Range
2.25 mm	1
2.75 mm	2
3.25 mm	3
3.5 mm	4
3.75 mm	5
4 mm	6
4.5 mm	7
5 mm	8
5.5 mm	9
6 mm	10
6.5 mm	10½
8 mm	11
9 mm	13
10 mm	15
12.75 mm	17
15 mm	19
19 mm	35
25 mm	50

the importance of gauge

You've got your pattern, all the supplies, and loads of enthusiasm. The next step is to work up a swatch.

PHOTOGRAPHER: DEAN TANNER

Working a swatch and adjusting it so you are knitting to gauge is the most important habit to adopt as you enter the knitter's world. It's helpful to knit a swatch—a sample of the pattern—for every project you make, but it's mandatory when fit is crucial, as with sweaters, skirts, and hats.

The gauge for a project is always given with the instructions. It states the number of stitches to knit with a specific yarn and a specific size knitting needle recommended to achieve the desired results. For example, if the gauge for your project is 16 stitches = 4" using size 7 needles, you'll want to knit a swatch with the suggested yarn (or a suitable substitute) that's at least 20 stitches wide and 4" long on the recommended size 7 needles. Bind off the stitches or place them on a length of yarn so you can measure the width of the 16 stitches in the center of the swatch.

How tightly or how loosely you knit, plus the size of the needles, determines your tension and the size of your stitches. If the width measurement of 16 stitches in your swatch is more than the required 4", your tension is too loose. You should try knitting the swatch with smaller-size needles. If the width

measurement is less than 4", your tension is too tight, and you should knit with larger-size needles.

When making adjustments for your new swatch, keep the yarn and the swatch measurements the same. To correct your gauge, change only the needle size. Work the swatch with different-size needles until your sample matches the gauge recommended for your project.

TIP: When using a stitch-gauge tool, line up the knitted Vs inside the gauge window. Each V-shape is a stitch—do not count the upside-down Vs. Use the point of a knitting needle to move from the center of one stitch to the next. Count each stitch across the opening. Divide the number of stitches you've counted by the number of inches. (The one shown is 10÷2, or 5 stitches per inch.) To check the row gauge, count the Vs up the side of the opening.

casting on

Before you can begin knitting or purling, you must first create a base row of stitches on one of your needles. This is called casting on.

Gather your yarn and needles, find a comfortable chair in a cozy corner, and you're ready to begin your knitting adventure—by casting on.

When you "cast on," you place stitches on one of your knitting needles in preparation for knitting—and perhaps purling—successive rows. The first cast-on stitch you'll learn is a slip knot, followed by three methods for casting on the rest of the stitches.

slip knot

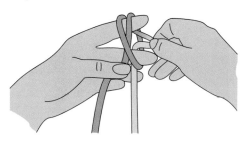

Leaving a 6" tail, * use your right hand to wrap the yarn *clockwise* around the index and middle fingers of your left hand, then drop the yarn strand behind those two fingers as shown in the illustration *above*; let your middle finger slip away from the work and pull the strand of yarn through the middle of the circle, forming a loop.

Place the loop on the needle and gently tug on the two strands to shape the knot. See the illustration *above*. For practice, take the stitch off the needle; make it two or three times more, repeating from *. Once you've mastered the slip knot, make a single knot on the needle and then try one of the cast-on methods that follows.

long tail cast-on I

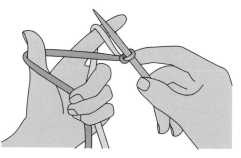

Estimate a yarn tail length that is three times the length of what the cast-on edge will be. Make a slip knot this distance from the yarn end and place it

on the right needle. * Referring to the illustration *bottom left,* position your thumb and index finger between the two strands of yarn (put the tail end over your thumb and the strand from the ball over your index finger); spread them apart. Close the other fingers into the palm of your hand and securely hold the yarn. Drop the needle position in your right hand (it should look like a sling shot).

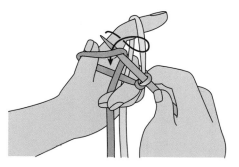

Moving in an *upward* direction, insert the needle *under* the yarn on the thumb and into the loop that's formed around the thumb. See the illustration *above*. Take the needle over the top of the yarn in front of your index finger and guide it down into the thumb loop—the strand of yarn from your index finger easily moves along with the needle. Pull the strand through the thumb loop, making a new loop on the right needle.

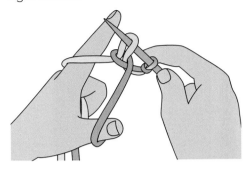

Drop the yarn around your thumb, and spread your index finger and thumb to tighten the loop on the needle—one cast-on stitch is made. As you spread your index finger and thumb, you're setting up your hand to begin the next cast-on stitch. Repeat from * (at the beginning of this method) to make a second cast-on stitch.

long tail cast-on 2

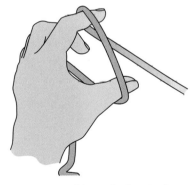

Estimate a yarn tail length that is three times the length of what the cast-on edge will be. * Holding the yarn in your left hand, wrap the tail end around your little finger and let it drop (you'll continue to feed the tail yarn into the cast-on row as you go). Wrap the ball yarn over your thumb, then over and under your index finger, forming a loop. See the illustration *above*.

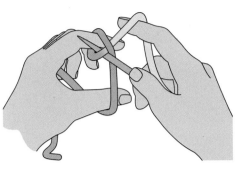

Hold the needle in your right hand. Referring to the illustration *above*, use the tip of the needle to draw the yarn from the bottom of the loop toward you.

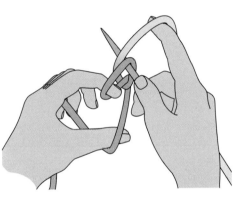

With your right hand, wrap the yarn *clockwise* over the top of the needle and then around and back to where it began, letting the strand fall over the top of the needle; hold it securely, slightly behind and to the right of the needle. See the illustration *above*.

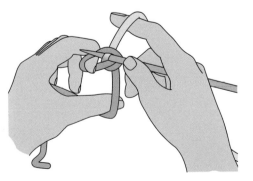

Use your left index finger to slip the loop over the wrapped strand of yarn and over the tip of the needle. Refer to the illustration *above*. Remove your

index finger; pull the yarn to tighten the loop. Repeat from * (at the beginning of this method) until the required number of stitches are cast on. Cast-on stitches will align at the bottom edge of the needle.

cable cast-on

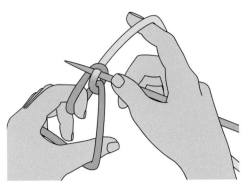

Make a slip knot on the left needle. With a second needle in your right hand, insert it into the slip knot front to back and wrap the ball yarn as if to knit. See the illustration *above*.

Pull the yarn through. Place the new loop from the right needle onto the left needle. See the illustration *above*. Two stitches are on the left needle.

* Insert the right needle between the slip knot and the first cast-on stitch. Knit a stitch; place the new loop on the left needle. Repeat from * to cast on the required number of stitches by working each successive stitch between the previous two stitches.

let's knit

Master just two basic stitches and the world of knitting is literally at your fingertips. Try the knit stitch first. Then go to the next page and learn how to purl.

PHOTOGRAPHER: DEAN TANNER

Start a practice swatch

by casting 20 stitches onto one needle (see *page 14,* or you could ask an experienced knitter to cast them on). Using the second (right) needle and following the instructions at *right,* begin knitting into the cast-on stitches—you will be creating new stitches on the right needle. Keep the yarn tension relaxed, and make the new stitches on the roundest part of each needle (past the tapered end) to create smooth, even stitches. Practice knitting for several rows.

When you knit every row, the pattern formed is called the garter stitch. An especially useful pattern, the resulting garter-stitch fabric lays flat, is reversible (identical on both sides), and has plenty of elasticity. You'll find entire scarves knitted in this pattern, afghans bordered with rows and rows of this stitch, and cardigans edged with it along the button and buttonhole bands.

garter stitch

1

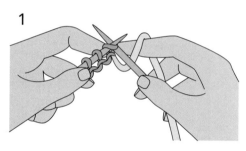

With the yarn in back, insert the right needle from the front to the back into the first stitch on the left needle. Notice that the right needle is positioned behind the left needle.

2

Form a loop by wrapping the yarn under and around the right needle.

3

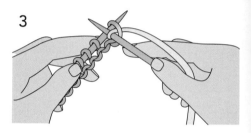

Pull the loop through the stitch so the loop is in front of the work.

4

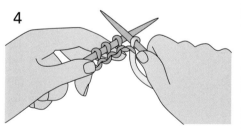

Slip the first or "old" knit stitch over and off the tip of the left needle, leaving it on the right needle.

Continue to practice by knitting five or six more rows.

now let's purl

You've got the knit stitch down pat. Are you ready to learn to purl?

PHOTOGRAPHER: DEAN TANNER

If you've practiced the knit stitch and made a garter-stitch swatch, you should be quite comfortable with the needles, the yarn, and your hands as they manipulate the two together. You also should be ready to learn to purl.

Think of the purl stitch as the reverse of the knit stitch. When you purl every row, you create the garter stitch, just as you do when you knit every row (see page 16). But use the knit and purl stitches together, and the knitting landscape is transformed into a myriad of textural patterns. For example, when you knit one row, then purl one row, and repeat these two rows over and over, you create one of the most familiar knitting patterns—the stockinette-stitch pattern, *below*.

stockinette stitch
knit side

purl side

To begin purling, start in the last row of your knit swatch and follow the instructions below.

1

With the yarn in front of the work, put the right needle from back to front into the first stitch on the left needle.

2

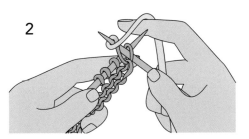

Form a loop by wrapping the yarn on top of and around the right needle.

3

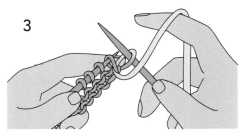

Pull the loop through the stitch to make a new purl stitch.

4

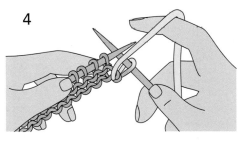

Slip the first or "old" purl stitch over and off the top of the left needle, leaving it on the right needle.

Practice purling by working garter stitch in purl (purl every row) for five or six more rows and then working stockinette stitch (knit one row, purl one row) for five or six rows.

here's how to make
ribbing

Ribbing—the stretchy band used for cuffs, collars, and waistlines—is a simple knit-and-purl pattern.

PHOTOGRAPHER: DEAN TANNER

Bands of ribbing worked into a knitted fashion behave much like the elastic that's stitched into a fabric garment. When you pull on it crosswise, it stretches, and when you release the tension, it resumes its original shape.

The knitting pattern most often used for sweater cuffs, hatbands, and the tops of socks and mittens is an alternating one of single knit and purl stitches worked across a row (knit one, purl one, knit one, purl one, and so on). See the example at *top right*.

The alternating stitches can also be worked double (knit, knit, purl, purl, knit, knit, purl, purl, and so on) to create the stretchy trim shown at *bottom right*.

Making ribbing is easy. Just remember that whenever you work knit and purl stitches in a series, you must bring the ball yarn to the back for knit stitches and to the front for purl stitches. The technique is quite rhythmic, so even though the passing of yarn from front to back and vice versa may seem awkward at first, it will become virtually automatic with a little practice.

Soon you'll learn to recognize the appearance of knit and purl stitches. This is particularly helpful when turning your work over to begin a new row of ribbing. A tiny "bead" juts out at the base of the purl stitch. The knit stitch is a V-shape. When you turn your work over to continue the rib pattern, always purl the purl stitches and knit the knit stitches as they face you.

knit 1, purl 1 ribbing

knit 2, purl 2 ribbing

adding a
ball of yarn

At some point in your project, you may need to add a ball of yarn. These tips explain how.

PHOTOGRAPHER: DEAN TANNER

Permanent knots are

a no-no in knitting. Here are a few suggestions to help you deal with these "knotty" issues.

● Always leave a 6" tail on both the joining and ending yarns. You may loosely knot them together at the ends so they don't unravel. However, when the work is completed, undo the knots and weave the ends into the finished piece.

● Join a new ball of yarn at the *beginning of a row* when the edge will be seamed. As you get close to the end of a ball, determine if you have enough yarn to complete the next row. To do this, you need to allow 1" per stitch when working on larger needles (size 8 and up) and ½" per stitch for smaller needles (size 7 and lower), and then add about 4" more to this measurement. If you don't have enough yarn, drop the yarn in use and begin the row with the new ball. After a few stitches, loosely knot the two tails together. When the work is completed, undo the knots; weave the ends into the finished piece.

● Join a new ball in the *middle of the row* when you want to keep the side edges straight and even (on a scarf, for example). To add the new ball, lay approximately 6" of the new yarn across

the front of the work and then knit the next two stitches with the new and old strands held together (see photo 1, *top right*); drop the old strand, and continue knitting with the yarn from the new ball (see photo 2, *bottom right*). When the work is finished, weave the ends into the piece.

● When doing circular knitting, join a new ball at any place in the round when the color stays the same. Attach the new ball in the same way as joining a new ball in the middle of the row (refer to the technique above).

● When changing yarn colors for striped patterns, always attach balls of new yarn near the beginning of a row or round. Simply cut the yarn from the old ball, leaving a 6" tail; then pick up the new yarn, again leaving a 6" tail, and continue knitting. When the work is finished, weave the ends into the piece. To keep the edges even when knitting in rows, knit the first one or two stitches with the old color, then join the new color in the next stitch.

● Sometimes in the middle of a row or round, you'll have a color change. In this instance, just begin knitting with the new color. Loosely knot the tails of the two strands together. When the piece is

finished, undo the knot. Adjust the tensions of those stitches close to the join, and weave the ends in the back of the work in the direction that allows the stitches to retain their correct shapes.

increasing stitches

When you knit increases into your work, you're adding stitches to the piece and making it larger. Sometimes you'll work increases simultaneously at or near both edges of a piece, and you'll want the resulting stitches to slant to the right at one edge and to the left on the other. At times, you'll want to give fullness to the whole piece, such as gathers at a skirt waistline, and you'll work increases evenly spaced across a row or round. There also may be times when you'll make arbitrary increases to set the work up for beginning a new pattern on the next row, and you'll want these increases to be invisible. Use the following increase methods to shape your work on the right (knit) side in the stockinette pattern.

TIP: If you are working M1 increases on the purl side of your work, work the stitch just as you would a knit-side increase, except purl the strand either through the front loop (to slant to the right) or the back loop (to slant to the left).

make one (M1)—version A
increased stitch slants to the right

Insert the tip of the left needle from *back to front* under the strand that lies between the next stitch on the left needle and the last stitch worked on the right needle. See the illustration *above*.

Referring to the illustration *above*, insert the right needle from *left to right* into the *front loop* of the lifted strand, and knit it from this position.

make one (M1)—version B
increased stitch slants to the left

Insert the tip of the left needle from *front to back* under the strand that lies between the first stitch on the left needle and the last stitch worked on the right needle. See the illustration *above*.

Referring to the illustration *above*, knit the strand on the left needle, inserting the needle from *right to left* into the *back loop*.

TIP: Another way to work an increase is to knit into the front and then into the back of the same stitch. To do this, knit the stitch to the point where you have the loop on the right needle, but do not remove the stitch from the left needle. Knit (from right to left) into the back loop of the same stitch to make a second loop, and then slide the stitch from the left needle.

decreasing stitches

Just as increasing the number of stitches in your knitting helps form the finished shape, so does decreasing. When you make decreases, you eliminate stitches that already are on your work. Whenever possible, it's better (and easier) to work decreases—and increases—on the right (knit) side in the stockinette pattern.

The following instructions will show you how to decrease. When you are making simultaneous paired decreases at or near each edge, you'll want one to slant to the right and the other to the left.

knit two together (k2tog)—

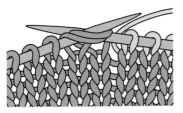

decreased stitch slants to the right
Working from *left to right* at the point of the decrease, insert the tip of the right needle into the second and then the first stitch on the left needle; knit the two stitches together as shown in the illustration *above*.

purl two together (p2tog)—
decreased stitch slants to the right

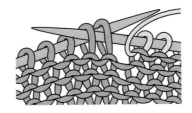

Working from *right to left* at the point of the decrease, insert the tip of the right needle into the first two stitches on the left needle and purl the two stitches together. See the illustration *above*.

slip, slip, knit (ssk)—

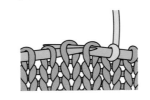

decreased stitch slants to the left
As if to knit, slip the first two stitches from the left needle, one at a time, to the right needle as shown *above*.

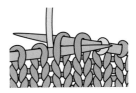

Insert the left needle into these two stitches from *back to front* as shown *above*, and knit them together from this position.

TIP: What it means to "slip" a stitch: When you slip a stitch, you simply move the stitch from one needle to the other without working it. Always slip stitches as though you are going to purl them, unless the instructions direct you otherwise (as in the ssk instructions at left).

When working decreases on the knit side, always slip stitches knitwise. When working decreases on the purl side, always slip the stitches purlwise.

TIP: Sometimes instructions call for the "psso" (pass the slipped stitch over) technique to work decreases. The resulting stitch slants to the left, like the ssk method above. Here's how it works: Slip the next stitch knitwise from the left needle to the right one; knit the next stitch on the left needle; insert the tip of the left needle into the slipped stitch and lift it over the knitted stitch.

binding off

When you finish a knitting project, the stitches are still on the needle. Binding off removes them and prevents them from unraveling.

Now that you've

practiced knitting, purling, increasing, and decreasing stitches, you may be asking, "How do I get the stitches off my needles?"

The technique for removing knitting from needles is called "binding off" or sometimes "casting off," and it means that the stitches will remain intact and not unravel once they are removed. Stitches can be bound off knitwise, purlwise, or in a pattern.

When binding off, you'll want to keep the bound-off edge as elastic as the knitted piece. You may find it helpful to use a larger right needle (two sizes larger). Instructions usually read "bind off," and it's a good idea to follow the stitch pattern for the piece you are making.

binding off knitwise

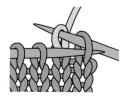

Loosely *knit* the first two stitches of the row or round.

Taking the needle along the *front* of the work, * insert the tip of the left needle into the first stitch on the right needle as shown *above*.

Lift the first stitch over the second stitch and drop the lifted stitch from the needle. See the illustration *above*.

One stitch remains on the right needle. See the illustration *above*.

Knit the next stitch on the left needle. Repeat from * until all stitches are bound off and one stitch remains on the right needle. Cut the yarn, pull the end through the stitch, and drop it from the needle.

binding off purlwise

Loosely *purl* the first two stitches of the row or round as shown *above*.

Taking the left needle along the *back* of the work, * insert the tip of the needle into the first stitch. Lift the first stitch over the second stitch and drop it from the needle. See the illustration *above*.

One stitch remains on the right needle. See the illustration *above*.

Purl the next stitch on the left needle. Repeat from * until all stitches are bound off and one stitch remains on the right needle. Cut the yarn, pull the tail through the stitch, and drop it from the needle.

Sometimes instructions will advise you to work the 3-Needle Bind-Off method instead of one of the more traditional binding-off methods described above. The 3-Needle Bind-Off finishes off a piece and also joins two pieces of knitting together, producing a seam that is firm and resistant to stretching. This method is used most often to join front and back pieces at the shoulders. For best results, you must have pieces with the same number of stitches on each of the two needles.

Note: These stitches often are placed on stitch holders while another piece of the project is knitted. When the two pieces are completed, they are bound off and seamed together using a single technique.

3-needle bind-off

With the right sides of two knitting pieces facing, hold the two needles together as one in the left hand with the tips pointed to the *right*.

Using a third needle of the same size, knit together one stitch from each needle. See the illustration *above*.

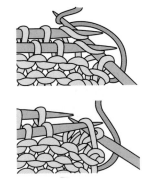

* Knit together the next stitch from each needle, pass the first stitch worked over the second stitch to bind off; repeat from * across to bind off all stitches. See the two illustrations *above*.

TIP: Binding off has multiple uses. It is a technique for decreasing stitches at armhole edges, shaping shoulders and necklines, and working buttonholes. In these instances, you are not finishing off the work but are instead using the technique to enhance the shape of the piece.

dealing with mistakes

Whether you're a beginner or an accomplished knitter, you'll likely make occasional mistakes in your work. Learning how to fix them is key.

Even accomplished

knitters make mistakes, but you'll never see them! These capable needleworkers haven't concocted secret methods for hiding a dropped stitch, a backward cable, or a big hole; they simply understand the impact errors have on a finished piece. They've learned how to make the necessary repairs and, most importantly, are willing to spend the time to make their project right.

Accept the fact that you, too, will make mistakes, and then try to do everything possible to correct any errors you find in your projects.

This doesn't mean you have to rip out and start at the beginning each time. There are ways to return to an error and correct it. If you're lucky, the mistake may have occurred only a stitch or two back, but it also may have happened many rows earlier.

Here are several common mistakes knitters make and the recommendations for fixing them.

fixing an incorrect stitch

Oftentimes, you'll find an error in your work just a few stitches back. To return to the error, simply unravel the piece stitch by stitch as follows:

To unravel knit stitches one at a time, *hold the yarn in your right hand at the *back* of the work. Tug gently on the yarn and angle it to the left: a hole will appear. Insert the tip of the left needle into the hole (it's the stitch in the row below the needle stitch). Drop the stitch on the right needle and pull lightly on the yarn to unravel or disengage it. Repeat from * across the row to the error. Correct the stitch and resume knitting.

Unravel purl stitches the same way, except hold the yarn in your right hand at the *front* of the work.

fixing an incorrect stitch several rows back

You can unravel rows of stitches by completely removing the work from the needles, pulling on the yarn, and unraveling the stitches to the error. Once you reach the error, place the stitches back on the needle, fix the error, and resume knitting.

Suggestions to help you make this type of repair follow.

unraveling rows of stitches from the knit side

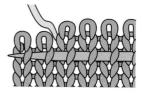

One way to avoid dropping stitches before you unravel the work is to take a smaller needle and weave it under the first loop of the knit stitch, over the second loop, under the third, and continue weaving across the row. See the illustration *above*.

unraveling rows of stitches from the purl side

You can do the same on the purl side as for the knit side (see the instructions above, except weave the small needle under the first loop of the *purl* stitch, over the second loop, under the third, and then continue weaving across the row). See the illustration *above*.

returning knit stitches to the needle

Keeping the ball yarn to the *left* of the work, return the stitches to the needle by inserting the needle from the *back of the stitch to the front*.

returning purl stitches to the needle

Keeping the ball yarn to the *left* of the work, return the stitches to the needle by inserting the needle from the *back of the stitch to the front*.

correcting dropped stitches

You may notice you have one less stitch in your work, and when you turn it over, a stitch (or loop) appears to be traveling down your work. Unravel back to the place in the same row where you are working.

ladder pickup on knit side of work

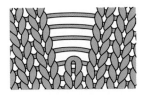

Notice the horizontal strands between the rows in the illustration *bottom left*. The dropped stitch has slid through these strands and traveled down the work.

Note: When picking up a dropped knit stitch, make sure the horizontal strands fall behind the dropped stitch.

Insert a crochet hook through the front of the dropped stitch and draw the strand through the dropped loop.

Continue up the work, pulling the strand through each loop one at a time until you get to the row where you are working. Slip the last loop on the left needle, knit it, and continue with your project.

ladder pickup on the purl side of the work

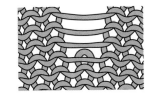

Notice the horizontal strands between the rows in the illustration *above*. The dropped stitch has slid off these strands as it traveled down the work.

Insert a crochet hook from the *back* of the dropped stitch and draw the strand through the dropped loop, *above right*. Continue up the work, pulling the strand through each loop one at a time until you get to the row where you are working. Slip the last loop on the left needle, purl it, and continue with your project.

Note: Make sure the horizontal strands are in front of the dropped purl stitch.

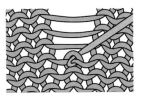

handling twisted stitches

As you work or make corrections to your knitted piece, you may find you've accidentally placed stitches backward on the needles. You can easily recognize when this occurs—the back loop of both a knit and a purl stitch will be ahead of the front loop of the stitch as it sits on the needle.

It's easy to correct this mistake by just knitting or purling into the back loop of each backward stitch.

abbreviations

Knitting instructions—filled with repetitious words and numbers—are cumbersome and can be challenging to read. Over time, a common abbreviated language has evolved, providing the knitter a kind of shorthand that makes following instructions much easier. The abbreviations used throughout this book—plus other common ones—are listed below. They may vary slightly from those used in other publications. A list of standard abbreviations from the Craft Yarn Council can be found at www.yarnstandards.com.

approx	approximately
beg	begin(ning)(s)
cn	cable needle
dec	decrease
dpn	double-pointed needle(s)
est	established
inc	increase
k or K	knit
kwise	as if to knit
k2tog	knit two stitches together (right-slanting decrease when right side facing)
M1	make one stitch; knit into back loop of running stitch
p or P	purl
pat	pattern
pm	place marker
psso	pass slipped stitch over
p2sso	pass two slipped stitches over
p2tog	purl two stitches together (right-slanting decrease when right side facing)
pwise	as if to purl
rem	remain(s)(ing)
rep	repeat(s)(ing)
rnd(s)	round(s)
RS	right side of work
sl	slip

sm	slip marker
ssk	(slip, slip, knit) slip two stitches, one at a time knitwise, insert left needle and knit two together (left-slanting decrease when right side facing)
ssp	(slip, slip, purl) slip two stitches, one at a time knitwise, pass back to left needle, purl together through back loops (left-slanting decrease when right side facing)
st(s)	stitch(es)
St st	stockinette stitch (knit one row, purl one row)
tbl	through the back loop(s)
tog	together
WS	wrong side of work
wyib	with yarn in back
wyif	with yarn in front
yo	yarn over
yon	yarn over needle
yrn	yarn around needle
( )	work instructions within parentheses in the place directed
[ ]	work step in brackets the number of times indicated
*	repeat the instructions following the single asterisk as directed

reading project
schematics

Before you begin any knitted garment, study the schematic drawings included with the instructions. You can adapt them to personalize your project.

If you've looked at any garment instructions in this publication, you've probably noticed the scaled illustrations, called schematics, that accompany them. The drawings, labeled with detailed measurements for each garment size, represent the flat, unassembled pieces (see the examples at right). The first number is for the smallest size. The numbers in parentheses are for alternate sizes.

The schematics aren't necessary for determining the garment size you want to make. (The chest measurement —taken around the chest at the underarm—is the most important factor for that.) However, the drawings will show you the measurements you should get when working to gauge. And they're useful when you want to make pattern alterations, such as lengthening the arm from wrist to underarm.

Schematics also can help you visualize the individual shapes of the garment pieces (sleeves, front, and back) as you knit them, and the schematics serve as guides when blocking the pieces to the desired

measurements. Remember, the shapes are representational—the actual tapering as you knit might look different. Study the schematics for your pattern before you begin, and then mark any necessary adjustments to create the best fit possible.

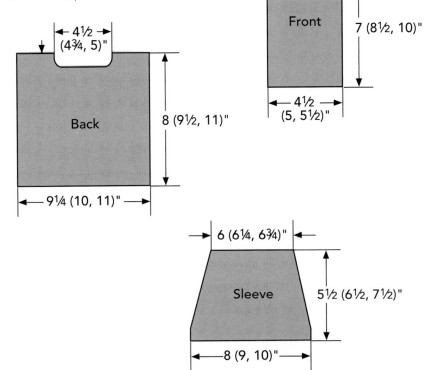

putting it all **together**

You've completed all the pieces for your knitting project. The only thing left to learn is how to put them neatly together.

PHOTOGRAPHER: DEAN TANNER

A pullover, a cardigan

with buttonholes and buttons, and even an afghan knitted in strips have something in common other than just knitting stitches: They're all designed in pieces and need to be assembled.

beyond the rectangle

Knitting your first sweater usually is a scary challenge, unless the sweater is a straight rectangle without shaping! So, as you work your way through your first sweater pattern that requires shaping (increasing for the sleeves and decreasing for the armholes and

neckline), you might discover that sometimes the directions don't tell you which decrease to use, only that you need to decrease at the beginning and the end of the row. Follow our tips for shaping, and you'll always have a great-looking project.

As you continue to grow in your knitting skills and you venture beyond making a rectangle (for a scarf, rug, or place mats), you'll learn additional techniques that will help you become more comfortable reading and interpreting knitting patterns. The following tips should give you a better understanding of what the instructions mean as you knit your first sweater.

shaping the sweater back

When knitting a sweater, the instructions usually start with the sweater back. Often the sweater back is worked from the bottom up, and you will work as instructed until you reach the armhole shaping. Begin the right armhole bind-off on a right side row and the left armhole bind-off on a wrong side row. In subsequent rows, use left-slant decreases along the right armhole and right-slant decreases along the left armhole. The neckline shaping usually has right-slant decreases along the right neckline edge and left-slant decreases along the left.

Although these decrease methods are not hard-and-fast rules to follow, they can be applied successfully in most cases. However, if the pattern you're using gives specific instructions for increasing and decreasing, follow those instructions.

The back neck stitches are either bound off or slipped onto a stitch holder and picked up later to finish the neckline. Binding off the back neck stitches will stabilize the garment and help prevent the fabric from stretching. This is especially true when working with dense, non-elastic fibers or heavyweight yarns.

shaping the pullover front

A pullover front is worked in the same manner as the back, except that at some point the instructions usually direct the knitter to make a few changes that apply to the neckline. These changes will be specifically written in the pattern for the front.

shaping cardigan fronts

When it comes to cardigan fronts, you might encounter the phrase "Work as for left (or right) front, reversing all shaping." Because one front has detailed instructions and the second doesn't, this phrase might puzzle you. Here are some tips you'll find helpful.

left front

The center left front edge is at the end of right-side rows (beginning of wrong-side rows). The armhole bind-off begins on a right side row, and left-slant decreases complete the armhole shaping. The neckline bind-off begins on a wrong side row followed by right-slant decreases.

right front

The center right front edge is at the beginning of right-side rows (end of wrong-side rows). The armhole bind-off begins on a wrong-side row, and right-slant decreases complete the shaping. The neckline bind-off begins on a right side row followed by left-slant decreases.

picking up stitches

Before picking up or seaming stitches, wet or dampen garment pieces to block them to the desired measurements and allow the pieces to dry. When the pieces are blocked, the edges lie flatter, and it's easier to work the stitches and rows.

Pick up stitches with the right (outer) side facing you, using either a crochet hook or a knitting needle. Use a smaller-size needle than planned for the border pattern (ribbing, for example), changing needles when the border begins. Join the yarn, and knit or purl the picked-up stitch. Across horizontal edges, pick up each "live" or bound-off stitch in the first row below the bind-off row. Along vertical edges, such as an armhole or

the front band, pick up the whole stitch (unless you are instructed otherwise), working two stitches every three rows, or three stitches every four rows. For a diagonal or curved pick-up, as in a crew or V neckline, pick up the stitches one-for-one until the edge becomes vertical, and then use the same pick-up ratio planned for the front edges.

seaming
invisible vertical seam

Sometimes called the ladder or mattress stitch, the invisible vertical seam is a good seam to use for sides and sleeves. To work the stitches, thread a yarn needle with the garment yarn or an appropriate seaming thread (if the main yarn is unsuitable for sewing). Working with right sides up, anchor the two cast-on edges together by making a figure-eight shape with the yarn. See illustration A, *below left*. Begin the seam by * inserting the yarn needle under the running bar between the first two stitches on one piece. Pull the yarn through, and repeat from * on the other piece of work. Alternate back and forth between each piece. Insert the yarn needle under one bar, working row by row, or under two running bars. The

seam tension should match your row gauge, and the finished seam should be able to withstand the garment's intended use.

There are several variations of this technique. See illustration B, *below center,* for one variety.

invisible vertical-to-horizontal seam (joins bound-off stitches to rows)

The invisible vertical-to-horizontal seam is used to attach sleeves to armholes. With a threaded yarn needle, insert the needle under the first leg of the first stitch beneath the bound-off edge (coming up through the stitch center). * Insert the needle under one horizontal bar between the first and second stitches of the sweater body; then insert the needle under the next two legs of the stitches beneath the bound-off edge **. Repeat from * to ** until the pieces are joined. Because this method attaches stitches to rows (with differing gauges), occasionally you'll need to work under two horizontal bars to keep the pieces even. See illustration C, *below right.*

invisible horizontal seam

Lay both the back and front sections flat, right side up, and with the corresponding stitches aligned.

Join the yarn to the right edge; with the threaded needle and working in the first row under the bind-off row, insert the needle under one leg of the first

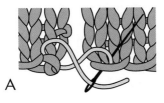

A

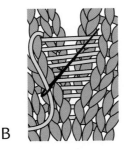

B

C

stitch on the front piece (coming up through the stitch center); * then insert the needle under both legs of the first stitch adjacent to the bind-off on the back piece. Insert the needle under the next two legs of the front stitch **.

D

Repeat from * to ** across the shoulder. See illustration D, *above*.

Garments with sleeves require stable shoulder seams capable of supporting the sleeve weight. To determine which seaming method works best for your sweater, consider the stitch pattern, yarn weight, and garment size. The invisible horizontal seam is an excellent and common one used for shoulder seaming.

Note: Another way to join the shoulders of a sweater is to use the 3-Needle Bind-Off. This is a technique that binds off and joins two pieces together in one action. See page 23. It shouldn't be used for garments made in heavyweight yarn.

attaching sleeves

When attaching sleeves to the body, sew the shoulder seams first. Fold the sleeve in half lengthwise, and place a stitch marker at the center top of the sleeve. On each side of center, place another stitch marker halfway down the sleeve. Place corresponding stitch markers along the body armhole halfway between the shoulder seam and the armhole bind-off. Matching all markers, pin the pieces together. Thread the needle with yarn and attach the sleeves to the body.

making cardigan front bands

Front bands are made horizontally or vertically; the instructions usually tell you which band to make.

The horizontal band is worked at right angles to the main body—joining stitches to rows. Pick up the required stitches along the front edge and work back and forth in pattern for the desired width, and then bind off.

Although instructions usually specify the number of stitches to pick up, if your gauge varies or you've altered the pattern, those numbers won't work. Before you start a horizontal band, work the border pattern along the edge of your gauge swatch to help you determine the best pick-up ratio.

A vertical band is normally worked in the same direction as the garment. The following are two easy methods: 1) Make bands separately and stitch them to the fronts during the finishing. 2) Cast on the band stitches with the front ribbing; when the ribbing is finished, place the band stitches on holders. To finish either kind of band, add one stitch for seaming, complete the band, and sew it to the front.

planning button and buttonhole placement

The first and last buttons are usually placed ½" to 1" from the top and lower edges, and the remaining buttons are spaced equally apart between them. You may need to modify the spacing or add an extra button or two to keep the bands from gaping open. A woman's cardigan has buttons on the left band and buttonholes on the right. A man's cardigan has buttons on the right band, buttonholes on the left.

Whenever possible, make your button band before the buttonhole band. Position the upper and lower buttons, and place the other buttons, evenly spaced, where you want them. Count the rows or stitches between the top and bottom buttons.

For a vertical band, divide the number of rows by the number of spaces between the buttons. For a horizontal band, divide the number of stitches by the number of spaces between the buttons. If the numbers don't divide evenly, use the extra rows or stitches before the first button or after the last one. A tape measure isn't a good tool for this job—count the stitches or rows instead. Mark each button position with a pin or colored thread.

making buttonholes

Align each buttonhole placement with its corresponding button marker. Try to start and end the buttonholes where they are less visible, usually the purl stitch in ribbing. Knitting stretches, so make the buttonholes slightly smaller than the button size. Remember to include how many rows or stitches each buttonhole will use.

In single ribbing (knit 1, purl 1), the eyelet buttonhole worked in a center purl stitch is almost invisible. Begin on a right side row; work to the buttonhole placement and then work a yarn over, knit two stitches together, and finish the row in the pattern. On the next row, work the yarn over as a regular stitch.

In a vertical band of knit 2, purl 2 ribbing, this same buttonhole can be worked with two purl stitches at the center of the right side rows. Work to the first center purl stitch, purl one, yarn over, knit two stitches together (one purl stitch, one knit stitch); finish the row. Different yarn weights change buttonhole size; the eyelet works well in thick or thin yarns.

The easiest buttonhole for a horizontal band and for larger buttonholes is a two-row buttonhole. It is worked as follows: Right side row—work to buttonhole placement, bind off the buttonhole stitches; finish the row. Next row—work to within one stitch of the buttonhole; work the front and back loop of the same stitch. Cast on one less stitch than the number bound off; finish row.

decreasing

Although decreases usually are made on right side rows, they sometimes occur on wrong side rows. The following are some general examples:
■ Right-slanting decrease: On right side rows, knit two together (k2tog). Use purl two together (p2tog) on wrong side rows.
■ Left-slanting decrease: The slip, slip, knit (ssk) is used on right side rows. Use slip, slip, purl (ssp) on wrong side rows.
■ Work decreases at least one stitch in from the edges to maintain even edges for seaming or picking up stitches. (See the Glossary at right.)

GLOSSARY FOR DECREASING

Knit two together (k2tog): A single decrease, with the facing stitch (the one on top) slanting right.

Working from front to back, insert the right needle knitwise into the second, then the first stitch on the left needle. Knit both stitches together.

Purl two together (p2tog): A single decrease, slanting to the right when viewed from the knit side.

With the purl side of the work facing you, insert the right needle purlwise through the first two stitches on the left needle. Purl both stitches together.

Slip, slip, knit (ssk): A single decrease, with the facing stitch slanting left.

Slip the first two stitches knitwise, one at a time, from the left needle to the right needle. Insert the left needle tip into the fronts of both stitches, from left to right, and knit them together.

Slip, slip, purl (ssp): A single decrease, slanting to the left when viewed from the knit side.

With the purl side of the work facing you, slip two stitches knitwise, one at a time, from the left needle to the right needle. Return the slipped stitches to the left needle, purlwise. Purl both stitches together through the back loops.

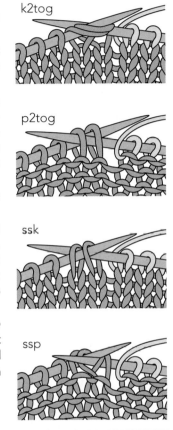

k2tog

p2tog

ssk

ssp

TIPS FOR SELECTING BUTTONS
■ To create the proper buttonhole size, buy the buttons before you start the buttonholes.
■ Buttons are made with or without a shank. Shank buttons are suitable for all yarn weights and are the best choice for thick, bulky knits.
■ Take your gauge swatch with you when buying buttons; it's a better visual than a skein of yarn.
■ Glassy, glittery buttons work well with dressy yarns. Bone, wood, and metal buttons are better choices for heavier, casual, or outdoor garments.
■ Buy washable buttons if you plan to wash the garment and dry-cleanable ones if the garment requires dry cleaning. Pay attention to the care instructions that come with the buttons.
■ If you can't find a good color match, choose a contrasting color.

knittingprojects

now that you can handle **the basics,** it's time to select a project. This collection, geared especially for the first-time knitter, is packed with easy-to-knit fashions, home accessories, and gifts. Take a look, be inspired, and get started!

easy-close accent

Keep this neck warmer snug by tucking one tail through the jumbo slit in the other.

DESIGNER: KENNITA TULLY
PHOTOGRAPHER: PERRY STRUSE

You can wrap up this design quickly with a single skein of bulky-weight yarn worked in Garter stitch (knit every row).

skill level
Beginner

finished measurements
Approx 6×34"

yarn
Lion Brand Homespun (Art. 790); 98% acrylic/2% polyester; 6 oz. (170 g); 185 yds. (167 m); bulky weight
● 1 skein #338 Nouveau

needles & extras
● Size 10 (6.5 mm) needles *or size needed to obtain gauge*
● Two stitch holders
● Blunt-end yarn needle

gauge
12 sts and 21 rows = 4" (10 cm) over Garter st (k every row).
TAKE TIME TO CHECK YOUR GAUGE.

instructions
Loosely cast on 21 sts and work in Garter st for approx 27".
K across the first 11 sts and place rem 10 sts on the stitch holder. K the 11 sts for approx 4" and place on the other stitch holder. Cut the yarn.
Sl the 10 sts from the first holder back onto the needle, join the yarn, and work until it's the same length as the right side of the slit. Place the sts from the 2nd holder onto the needle and cont in Garter st for 3 more inches. Loosely bind off all sts. Weave in the ends.

faux-fur flair

Look what happens when exotic "fur" yarn meets up with a simple knitted triangle!

DESIGNER: CANDACE EISNER STRICK
PHOTOGRAPHER: PERRY STRUSE

skill level
Beginner

finished measurement
Center back length = 12"

yarns
Lion Brand Fun Fur (Art. 320); 100% polyester; 1¾ oz. (50 g); 64 yds. (58 m); bulky weight
● 2 balls #153 Black (A)
● 1 ball #113 Red (B)

needle & extra
● Size 10.5 (6.5 mm) 29" circular needle *or size needed to obtain gauge*
● Blunt-end yarn needle

gauge
16 sts and 32 rows = 4" (10 cm) worked over Garter st (k every row).
TAKE TIME TO CHECK YOUR GAUGE.

Notes: Knit into back of single yarn overs (yos) from Row 1 of pattern. When working in yos at ends of Rows 1 and 2, knit into front of first yo; knit into back of second yo. Be sure to mark right side of your work. Cut yarn at each color change; weave in ends as you go.

instructions
With A, cast on 2 sts, place marker (pm), cast on 1 st (center st), pm, cast on 2 sts—5 sts. K 1 row.
Row 1 (RS): Yo twice, k to marker, yo, k center st, yo, k to end—9 sts.
Row 2: Yo twice, k to end of row—11 sts.

Note: Piece is inc by 6 sts every 2 rows.
Rep the above 2 rows 12 more times—83 sts.
Change to B and work the above 2 rows 4 times—107 sts.
Change to A and work the above 2 rows 6 times—143 sts.
Change to B and work the above 2 rows 2 times—155 sts.
Change to A and work the above 2 rows 3 times—173 sts.
Bind off loosely, making oversize loops with the yarn as you bind off.

This exciting accent has a designer look but not the price tag. Who would ever guess you made it—and in less than a day?

long & lean scarf

A scarf this long and lean makes you a standout in any crowd. So does its 3×3 rib pattern, knit in 12 terrific hues.

PHOTOGRAPHERS: PERRY STRUSE (*OPPOSITE*); DEAN TANNER (*RIGHT*)

skill level
Beginner

finished measurements
Approx 6×60"

yarns
Lion Brand Kool Wool (Art. 380); 50% merino wool/50% acrylic; 1¾ oz. (50 g); 60 yds. (54 m); bulky weight
- 1 skein #098 Ivory (A)
- 1 skein #124 Khaki (B)
- 1 skein #114 Denim (C)
- 1 skein #153 Black (D)
- 1 skein #146 Fuchsia (E)
- 1 skein #109 Royal Blue (F)
- 1 skein #149 Charcoal (G)
- 1 skein #186 Melon (H)
- 1 skein #130 Grass (I)
- 1 skein #147 Eggplant (J)
- 1 skein #113 Tomato (K)
- 1 skein #125 Camel (L)

needles & extra
- Size 10 (6 mm) needles *or size needed to obtain gauge*
- Blunt-end yarn needle

gauge
28 sts and 15 rows = 4" (10 cm) over st pat.
TAKE TIME TO CHECK YOUR GAUGE.

pattern stitch
3×3 Rib Pat
Row 1 and all WS rows: P3, *k3, p3, rep from * to end of row.
Row 2 and all RS rows: K3, *p3, k3, rep from * to end of row.
Rep Rows 1 and 2 for pat.

instructions
With A, loosely cast on 39 sts and work 3x3 Rib Pat for 36 rows. Attach B and cont in pat for 36 rows.
Cont working 36 rows of each color in alphabetical order. Bind off in pat. Weave in ends.

Styling this almost 10-foot-long scarf is truly a breeze. Loosely wrap it once around your neck, and let the colorful tails fall straight down past your knees!

wavy-rib warmer

Thirsty for a little more adventure in your knitting? You'll love the wavy-rib motif that comprises this scarf design.

DESIGNER: KENNITA TULLY
PHOTOGRAPHER: PERRY STRUSE

skill level
Beginner

finished measurements
Approx 4½×60"

yarn
Lion Brand Fishermen's Wool (Art. 150); 100% virgin wool; 8 oz. (224 g); 465 yds. (418 m); worsted weight
● 1 skein #098 Natural

needles & extra
● Size 9 (5.5 mm) needles *or size needed to obtain gauge*
● Blunt-end yarn needle

gauge
19 sts and 22 rows = 4" (10 cm) over pat st.
TAKE TIME TO CHECK YOUR GAUGE.

pattern stitch
Wavy Rib Pat
Rows 1, 3, 5, 13, 15, and 17: K3, *p2, k2; rep from *, end p2, k3.
Row 2 and All Even Rows: K the knit sts and p the purl sts.
Rows 7, 9, and 11: K3, *p6, k2; rep from *, end p6, k3.
Rows 19, 21, and 23: K3, p2, *k2, p6; rep from *, end k2, p2, k3.
Row 24: K the knit sts and p the purl sts.
Rep Rows 1–24 for pat.

instructions
Loosely cast on 28 sts and work Wavy Rib Pat until scarf measures approx 60", ending with Rows 1–6. Loosely bind off all sts in pat.

The movement of this wavy-patterned scarf shows off best when knitted in a light-color yarn. Wear it as shown *opposite* or with the reverse side on top as shown *above*.

variegated
place mats

Fast and easy to knit, these garter-stitch mats can add texture, color, and interest to your dining table. Choose shades of the sand, the sea, or maybe even the rainbow to complement your dishes.

DESIGNER: VAL LOVE
PHOTOGRAPHERS: SCOTT LITTLE
(*RIGHT*); ANDY LYONS (*OPPOSITE*)

Place mats make ideal first projects for beginners. Knit the ones shown here in Garter stitch, and watch them grow stunning with each changing band of color.

skill level
Beginner

finished measurements
Approx 12×16"

yarns
Classic Elite Provence; 100% mercerized cotton; 256 yds.; double knitting weight
For 4 mats:
- 2 hanks #2612 Lemon*
  OR #2681 Bright Chartreuse (A)
- 2 hanks #2679 Hydrangea Blossom*
  OR #2648 Slate Blue (B)

As we went to press, #2612 Lemon and #2679 Hydrangea Blossom had been discontinued; substitute similar or coordinating colors of your choice.

needles & extra
- Size 6 (3.75 mm) knitting needles *or size needed to obtain gauge*
- Blunt-end yarn needle

gauge
In Garter st (k all rows), 20 sts and 40 rows (20 ridges) = 4" (10 cm).
TAKE TIME TO CHECK YOUR GAUGE.

instructions
With A, cast on 60 sts. K all rows, changing color at beg of rows as follows (first row is RS):
12 ridges A, 1 ridge B
8 ridges A, 1 ridge B
6 ridges A, 1 ridge B
4 ridges A, 1 ridge B
2 ridges A, 1 ridge B
1 ridge A, 2 ridges B
1 ridge A, 4 ridges B
1 ridge A, 6 ridges B
1 ridge A, 8 ridges B
1 ridge A, 12 ridges B
Bind off. Weave loose ends into WS of work.

fringed
floor rug

Create the nubby surface of this garter-stitch floor mat by alternating two knit rows of natural yarn with two of sage. Easy! Then finish the ends in waves of slender fringe.

DESIGNER: LISA CARNAHAN
PHOTOGRAPHER: PERRY STRUSE

A pattern like this one can easily be adapted for place mats, a table runner, or a larger floor rug. Simply change the number of cast-on stitches and then follow the pattern stitch until you achieve the desired length.

skill level
Beginner

finished measurements
Approx 25×36", excluding fringe

yarns
Lion Brand Lion Cotton (Art. 760); 100% cotton; 5 oz. (140 g); 236 yds. (212 m); worsted weight
- 3 balls #181 Sage (A)
- 4 balls #098 Natural (B)

needles & extras
- Size 10 (6 mm) needles *or size needed to obtain gauge*
- Size G-6 (4 mm) or H-8 (5 mm) crochet hook (to attach fringe)
- Nonskid liquid or spray (optional)
- Blunt-end yarn needle

gauge
13 sts and 24 rows = 4" (10 cm) with double strand working Garter st (k every row).
TAKE TIME TO CHECK YOUR GAUGE.

pattern stitch
Stripe Pat
Note: Carry the color that's not in use up the side of the work, catching it in the end stitches of the color in use.
Rows 1 and 2: With double strand of B, knit.
Rows 3 and 4: With double strand of A, knit.
Rep Rows 1–4 for Stripe Pat.

instructions
With double strand of A, cast on 82 sts.
K 1 row.
Work in Stripe Pat until piece measures 36" long, ending with Row 3 of pat.
With a double strand of A, bind off all sts. Weave in ends.

finishing
Fringe: Wind B around a 4½" piece of cardboard 228 times. Cut in half along one edge of cardboard to make 9" lengths.

Using six strands per fringe, attach 19 fringes evenly spaced on both short sides of the rug by bringing the crochet hook through the knitted fabric, drawing a loop through the fabric, and then bringing the tails through the loop. Tighten the knot of the fringe by pulling on the tails. Trim the fringe ends evenly after all are attached. If desired, apply a nonskid product to the back of the rug.

striped throw

This handsome warmer is a great fall or winter project. Designed as a single piece, it'll keep you cozy even while you knit it.

DESIGNER: SARAH HARPER
PHOTOGRAPHER: PERRY STRUSE

skill level
Easy

finished measurements
Approx 46×62"

yarns
Lion Brand Chenille Thick & Quick (Art. 950); 91% acrylic/9% rayon; 100 yds. (90 m); super bulky weight
- 2 skeins #125 Chocolate (A)
- 1 skein #149 Grey (B)
- 1 skein #107 Periwinkle (C)

Lion Brand Wool-Ease Thick & Quick (Art. 640); 80% acrylic/20% wool; 6 oz. (170 g); 108 yds. (97 m); super bulky weight
- 4 skeins #404 Wood (D)
- 2 skeins #152 Pewter (E)
- 2 skeins #114 Denim (F)

needle & extra
- Size 13 (9 mm) 29" circular needle *or size needed to obtain gauge*
- Blunt-end yarn needle

gauge
9 sts and 12 rows = 4" (10 cm) over St st (k 1 row, p 1 row).
TAKE TIME TO CHECK YOUR GAUGE.

Note: When beginning and ending colors, leave at least a 10" tail so that they can be woven in later.

instructions
With D, cast on 105 sts, k 3 rows. Change to A and k 2 rows.
Rows 1 and 2: With A, k across.
Rows 3–14: With D, k4; work in St st (k RS rows, p WS rows) to last 4 sts; k4.
Rows 15 and 16: With A, k across.
Rows 17 and 18: With E, k across.
Rows 19 and 20: With B, k across.
Rows 21 and 22: With E, k across.
Rows 23 and 24: With C, k across.
Rows 25–32: With F, k4; work in St st to last 4 sts; k4.
Rows 33 and 34: With C, k across.
Rows 35 and 36: With E, k across.
Rows 37 and 38: With B, k across.
Rows 39 and 40: With E, k across.
Rep Rows 1–40 four more times. K 4 rows with A. Change to D and k 3 rows. Bind off all sts loosely. Weave in yarn tails. Block lightly.

Two textured yarns in an assortment of neutral hues make this simple project fun to knit and watch "grow." Make the throw longer, if you like, by adding an extra repeat of the four-band pattern.

A sampler of yarn colors (solids and prints) and weights (worsted, light bulky, bulky, and super bulky) ripples across this tactile design.

a classic ripple

Here's a quick-to-make ripple that will keep you luxuriously warm and cozy at home—or in the car. Combinations of six different yarns give the throw its rich shading and texture.

DESIGNER: ADINA KLEIN
PHOTOGRAPHER: PERRY STRUSE

skill level
Easy

finished measurements
Approx 43x55", excluding fringe

yarns
Lion Brand Homespun (Art. 790); 98% acrylic/2% polyester; 6 oz. (170 g); 185 yds. (167 m); bulky weight
● 1 skein #312 Edwardian (A)
● 1 skein #301 Shaker (B)
● 1 skein #311 Rococo (C)

*Lion Brand Jiffy (Art. 450); 100% acrylic; 3 oz. (85 g); 135 yds. (123 m); light bulky weight
● 3 balls #125 Taupe (F)

Lion Brand Chenille Thick & Quick (Art. 950); 91% acrylic/9% rayon; 100 yds. (90 m); super bulky weight
● 2 skeins #227 Desert Print (D)
● 2 skeins #125 Chocolate (E)

Lion Brand Wool-Ease (Art. 620); 80% acrylic/20% wool; solids = 3 oz. (85 g); 197 yds. (180 m); prints = 2.5 oz. (70 g); 162 yds. (146 m); worsted weight
● 1 ball #152 Oxford Grey (G)
● 2 balls #403 Mushroom (H)
● 2 balls #232 Woods Print (I)

Lion Brand Wool-Ease Chunky (Art. 630); 80% acrylic/20% wool; 5 oz. (140g); 153 yds. (140 m); bulky weight
● 1 ball #127 Walnut (J)

*Lion Brand Woolspun (Art. 370); 63% wool/26% acrylic/11% polyester; 100 yds. (90 m); bulky weight
● 3 skeins #124 Ecru (K)

*As we went to press, Jiffy yarn #125 Taupe had been discontinued; substitute a coordinating color. Woolspun yarn also had been discontinued; substitute a suitable bulky-weight yarn.

needle & extras
● Size 17 (12 mm) 29" circular knitting needle or size needed to obtain gauge
● Size 10½/K (6.5 mm) crochet hook
● Blunt-end yarn needle

gauge
In Body Pattern with a double strand of yarn, 9 sts and 12 rows = 4" (10 cm).
TAKE TIME TO CHECK YOUR GAUGE.

pattern stitch
Body Pat (a multiple of 16 sts + 1 st; a rep of 8 rows)

Row 1 (RS): K1, *yo, k6, (sl next 2 sts tog as if to knit, k1, pass the 2 slipped sts over the k1—double dec made), k6, yo, k1; rep from * across.
Row 2: Purl.
Row 3: Rep Row 1.
Row 4: Purl.
Rows 5–8: Knit.
Rep Rows 1–8 for Body Pat.

Notes: Throw is worked back and forth on a circular needle to accommodate large number of stitches; two yarn strands held together are used throughout.

striped color sequence
Stripe 1: A+G
Stripe 2: D+H
Stripe 3: Two strands F
Stripe 4: E+I
Stripe 5: Two strands K
Stripe 6: B+H
Stripe 7: C+I
Stripe 8: F+J
Work 4 rows of each stripe.

instructions
Beg at lower edge with Stripe 1, cast on 97 sts. K 3 rows for Garter st border. Work 4 rows each of Stripes 2–8. Rep 4 rows each of Stripes 1–8 for 4 more times. Knit 3 rows in Stripe 1 for Garter st border. Bind off all sts loosely.

finishing
Fringe (make 26): Cut 18"-long strands. Mix the yarns so that there are 18 strands for each fringe. Fold strands in half to form a loop. With wrong side facing and using a crochet hook, take loop through corner at one long end. Take ends through loop and pull up to form a knot. At each long edge, add 13 total fringe, placing them at tips and base of each point.

wardrobe
chic

Want to add knitted pizzazz to your wardrobe? No need to shop in stores selling designer labels— you can make something stylish yourself, like this versatile knit trio.

DESIGNER: VLADIMIR TERIOKHIN
PHOTOGRAPHER: PERRY STRUSE

skill level
Easy

finished size
One size fits most adults.

finished measurements
Capelet = 23" wide at lower edge;
13" long from shoulder
Fingerless gloves = 9½" long
Hat circumference = 20"

yarns
Lion Brand Homespun (Art. 790);
98% acrylic/2% polyester; 6 oz. (170 g);
185 yds. (167 m); bulky weight
• 1 skein #311 Rococo (A) for Capelet
• 1 skein #311 Rococo (A) for Hat
  and Fingerless Gloves

Lion Brand Fun Fur (Art. 320);
100% polyester; 1½ oz. (40 g); 57 yds.
(52 m); bulky weight
• 3 skeins #205 Sandstone (B) for
  Capelet
• 3 skeins #205 Sandstone (B) for Hat
  and Fingerless Gloves

needles & extras
• Size 10½ (6.5 mm) 24" circular needle
  for Capelet *or size needed to obtain
  gauge*
• Set of four size 10½ (6.5 mm) double-
  pointed needles (dpns)
• Stitch marker
• Two stitch holders
• Blunt-end yarn needle

gauge
8½ sts and 14 rows = 4" (10 cm) over St
st (k 1 row, p 1 row) using 1 strand each
of A and B held together.
TAKE TIME TO CHECK YOUR GAUGE.

*Notes: The Capelet and Fingerless
Gloves are worked using one strand
each of A and B held together; the Hat
is worked using one strand of A and two
strands of B. The Capelet is worked in
rounds from the bottom edge to the
shoulder shaping, then divided into
front and back and worked in rows; the
collar is worked in rounds on double-
pointed needles. The Hat and
Fingerless Gloves are worked in rounds
on double-pointed needles.*

capelet
Holding 2 strands of yarn tog (1 of A
and 1 of B) and using circular needle,
cast on 100 sts. Join in round, placing
marker (pm) at end of rnd.
Work 4 rnds in k1, p1 rib. K every rnd
until work measures 8½".
Shape sides—Rnd 1: *K2, ssk, k42,
k2tog,* k4; rep from * to * once; k2.

These elegant accessories—a capelet, fingerless gloves, and a hat—are accomplished using two specialty yarns.

Rnd 2: Knit.

Rnd 3: *K2, ssk, k40, k2tog,* k4; rep from * to * once; k2.

Rnd 4: K 1 rnd even.

Rnd 5: *K2, ssk, k38, k2tog,* k4; rep from * to * once; k2.

Rnd 6: K 1 rnd even. Cont to dec 4 sts on next and following alternate rnds as est until there are 68 sts.

Divide front and back—Next Row: Bind off 3 sts; k31, turn and leave rem sts unworked.

Cont in St st for back and bind off 3 sts at beg of next row, then 2 sts at beg of following 4 rows—14 sts. Place these sts on stitch holder.

With RS facing, join yarn to first unworked st on circular needle and work front same as back.

Collar: With RS facing and set of 4 dpns, k14 from back and front stitch holders—28 sts. Divide sts over 3 needles as follows: N1–10 sts; N2–10 sts; N3–8 sts. Join in round, pm before first stitch. Work 4½" in k1, p1 rib. Bind off loosely in rib. Weave in ends.

fingerless glove (make 2)

Holding 2 strands of yarn tog (1 of A and 1 of B) and using dpns, cast on 24 sts. Divide sts evenly over 3 needles. Join in round, pm on first st. Work 5 rnds in k2, p2 rib.

Shape thumb opening: Working back and forth across needles in rows, work 4 rows in k2, p2 rib. Beg working again in rnds of k2, p2 rib until glove measures 9½" long, or desired length. Bind off loosely in rib. Weave in ends.

hat

Holding 3 strands of yarn tog (1 of A and 2 of B) and using dpns, cast on 48 sts. Divide sts evenly over 3 needles. Join in round, pm before first stitch. Work 7" in k2, p2 rib.

Shape top—Rnd 1: *K2tog, p2; rep from * around—36 sts. Break off 2

strands of B and cont with 1 strand of A only.

Rnd 2: *K1, p2; rep from * around.

Rnd 3: *K1, p2tog; rep from * around—24 sts.

Rnd 4: *K1, p1; rep from * around.

Rnd 5: (K2tog) 12 times—12 sts. Cut yarn and draw through rem sts. Pull tight to close. Weave in ends.

toddler's
cardigan & hat

If you can knit a rectangle, you can outfit your toddler in this so-soft cardigan and hat.

DESIGNER: EDIE ECKMAN
PHOTOGRAPHER: DEAN TANNER

sizes
6 mos. (12 mos.)
Shown in Size 12 mos. When only one number is given, it applies to both sizes. *Note: For ease in working, circle all numbers pertaining to your size.*

finished measurements
Chest = 22 (25)"

yarn
Lion Brand Homespun Baby (Art. 800); 98% acrylic/2% polyester; 3 oz. (85 g); 93 yds. (85 m); bulky weight
• 4 (4) skeins #157 Sunshine

needles & extras
• Size 10½ (6.5 mm) needles *or size needed to obtain gauge*
• Blunt-end yarn needle
• Three ½"-diameter buttons

gauge
11 sts and 20 rows = 4" (10 cm) over Garter st (k every row).
TAKE TIME TO CHECK YOUR GAUGE.

Note: Use long-tail cast-on throughout.

cardigan
BACK
Cast on 30 (34) sts. Work Garter st until piece measures 11 (12)". Bind off.

FRONT (make 2)
Cast on 17 (19) sts. Work Garter st until piece measures 11 (12)". Bind off.

SLEEVE (make 2)
Cast on 26 (28) sts. Work Garter st until piece measures 5 (7)". Bind off.

finishing
Sew shoulder seams, leaving a 5 (5½)" neck opening. See top edge of Back diagram, *below.* Sew Sleeves onto body of cardigan. Fold cardigan at shoulders; sew side and underarm seams. Weave in ends.
Add buttons: Sew buttons on Right Front edge for a boy, Left Front edge for a girl, evenly spaced with bottom button 2" from lower edge and top button 4" from neck edge. To close the cardigan, pull buttons through fabric on opposite front edge. Fold back the lapels and tack.

hat
Cast on (20) 23 sts. Work Garter st until piece measures 12". Bind off loosely. Fold in half; seam the sides.
Make corner tassels: Wrap yarn 10 times around a 4" piece of cardboard. Cut one edge to make ten 8" lengths—a bundle of five for each corner. Fold one bundle in half and wrap some yarn around the top about 1" from fold; fluff out ends. Sew a tassel to one corner. Rep for other corner.

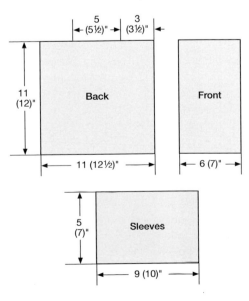

baby suite

Turn a basic cardigan, cap, and blanket into a playful set using big blocks and bold stripes of color. Make it for a boy as directed or in pistachio, pastel pink, white, and sunflower for a girl.

DESIGNER: BARBARA ALBRIGHT
PHOTOGRAPHER: PERRY STRUSE

skill level
Easy

size
3 (6, 12) months
The pattern is written for the smallest size with changes for larger sizes in parentheses. When only one number is given, it applies to all sizes.
Note: For ease in working the cardigan and cap, circle all numbers pertaining to the size you're making.

finished measurements
Cardigan chest (buttoned) = 18¼ (20, 22)"; length = 8 (9½, 11)"
Cap circumference = 17½ (18½, 19½)"
Blanket = Approx 32×33"

yarns
Lion Brand Kitchen Cotton (Art. 760); 100% cotton; 5 oz. (140 g); 236 yds. (212 m); worsted weight
● 2 balls #123 Seaspray (A)
● 2 balls #106 Pastel Blue (B)
● 2 balls #100 White (C)
● 2 balls #157 Sunflower (D)

needles & extras
● Size 4 (3.5 mm) knitting needles *or size needed to obtain gauge*
● One set size 4 (3.5 mm) double-pointed knitting needles (dpns) for cap
● Blunt-end yarn needle
● Stitch holders
● Ring-type stitch marker
● Four (five, six) ⅝"-diameter buttons

gauge
In St st (k 1 row, p 1 row), 20 sts and 30 rows = 4" (10 cm).
TAKE TIME TO CHECK YOUR GAUGE.

special techniques
3-Needle Bind-Off (cardigan shoulders): Holding RSs tog, with points of needles to the right, use a 3rd needle of the same size as follows: K tog 1 st from each needle. *K tog 1 st from each needle, pass first st over 2nd st to bind off; rep from * across until all sts are used. At end, cut working yarn and pull through last st to secure.

I-Cord (used for cap over last 5 sts): Using 2 dpns, k4 (4, 5) sts; do not turn. *Slide sts to opposite end of dpn; keeping yarn in back, k 4 (5, 5); rep from * for required length.

cardigan
BACK
Beg at lower edge with A, cast on 46 (50, 55) sts.
Rows 1–4: K 4 rows for Garter st border.
Next Row: Purl.
Next 49 (61, 73) Rows: Work in St st (k on RS, p on WS) until piece measures approx 7 (8½, 10)" from beg, ending with a WS row—54 (66, 78) total rows, including the Garter st border.
Shape shoulder and neck: K15 (16, 18) sts; join 2nd ball of A and bind off center 16 (18, 19) sts for back neck; with same ball, k to end. Working shoulders

at the same time and with separate balls, bind off 3 sts at each neck edge. Cont in St st on 12 (13, 15) sts until piece measures approx 8 (9½, 11)" from beg, ending with a RS row. Cut yarn, leaving a 12" tail, and place rem sts for each shoulder onto a holder.

LEFT FRONT
Beg at lower edge with B, cast on 24 (27, 29) sts. K 4 rows for Garter st border.
Row 5 (WS): K4, p to end.
Row 6 Buttonhole (RS): K across to last st; bind off 1 st, k last st.
Row 7 Buttonhole: K1, yo, k2, p to end.
Row 8: Knit.
Row 9: K4, p to end.
Row 10: Knit.
Rep Rows 9 and 10 for 0 (1, 2) more times. Cut B, leaving a 6" tail to weave in later.
Stripes: With C, rep Rows 9 and 10 for 5 (6, 7) times; fasten off, leaving a 6" tail. With B, rep Rows 9 and 10 for 5 (6, 7) times; fasten off, leaving a 6" tail. Rep these 20 (24, 28) rows for Stripes and at the same time, rep Buttonhole Rows 6 and 7 on Rows 20 and 21, 34 and 35, and 48 and 49 for all sizes.
For sizes 6 and 12 mos., rep Buttonhole Rows 6 and 7 on Rows 62 and 63.
For size 12 mos., rep Buttonhole Rows 6 and 7 on Rows 76 and 77. Work even in pat until piece measures approx 7 (8½, 10)" from beg, ending with a RS row.
Shape neck: Bind off the first 9 (11, 11) sts, p to end. K 1 row. At beg of next WS row, bind off 3 sts, p to end. Work

even on 12 (13, 15) sts to approx 8 (9½, 11)" from beg, ending with a WS row.
Join shoulder: With RS facing, return sts from back left shoulder holder to needle so that when holding WS of each piece tog, needles point toward armhole edge. Use 3-Needle Bind-Off to join shoulder sts. See Special Techniques, 3-Needle Bind-Off, page 54.

RIGHT FRONT
Beg at lower edge with A, cast on 24 (27, 29) sts. K 4 rows for Garter st border.
Body Pat—Row 5 (WS): P across to last 4 sts, k4.
Row 6: Knit.
Rep Rows 6 and 7 until piece measures approx 7 (8½, 10)" from beg, ending with a WS row.
Shape neck: Bind off 9 (11, 11) sts, k to end. P across. Bind off 3 sts, k to end. Work even in St st on 12 (13, 15) sts until piece measures approx 8 (9½, 11)" from beg, ending with a WS row.
Join shoulder: With RS facing, return sts from back right shoulder to needle so that needle points toward neck edge. Use 3-Needle Bind-Off to join shoulder sts.

RIGHT SLEEVE
Beg at the top with D, cast on 40 (45, 50) sts.
Rows 1–5: Beg with a p row, work 5 St st rows.
Row 6 (Dec Row): K2, k2tog, k across to last 4 sts, k2tog, k2.

Rep Rows 1–6 for 4 (6, 7) more times—30 (31, 34) sts. Work even until sleeve measures approx 5½ (6½, 7½)" from beg, ending with a RS row. Knit 4 rows. Bind off kwise.

LEFT SLEEVE
Beg at top edge with C, cast on 40 (45, 50) sts.
Work as for Right Sleeve except * work 10 (12, 14) rows with C ** and 10 (12, 14) rows with B.
Rep from * to ** again, then complete sleeve with B.

finishing
Place markers 4¼ (4¾, 5¼)" from shoulder seams and on each side edge. Set in sleeves between markers. Join underarm and side seams.
Neckband:
Note: When changing colors, bring new color strand from under present strand for a "twist" to prevent holes.
With RS facing, using C, and beg at right front neck edge, pick up and k16 (18, 18) sts evenly spaced to shoulder seam.
With A, pick up and k31 (33, 34) sts evenly spaced to shoulder seam and 16 (18, 18) sts evenly spaced on left neck edge. K 4 rows on the 63 (69, 70) sts. Bind off kwise. Sew buttons opposite buttonholes. Weave in tails on WS of fabric.

cap
Leaving a 6" tail and beg at lower edge using A, cast on 88 (92, 98) sts.
K 5 rows for Garter st border. Distribute sts onto 3 dpns. Place a marker to indicate beg of rnd; join and k every rnd until piece measures approx 1½ (1¾, 2)" from beg. With C, k every rnd for approx 1½ (1¾, 2)". With B, k every rnd for approx 1½ (1¾, 2)". Change to D and k 2 rnds.

Shape top: With D, k2tog around and around until 4 (5, 5) sts rem. Using 2 dpns, work I-Cord for 4". Cut yarn and thread tail through rem sts. Pull tight and secure in place. Tie I-Cord into an overhand knot. Seam the Garter st band. Weave in tails on WS of fabric.

blanket
STRIP 1
Block 1
Beg at the lower edge with A, cast on 80 sts. K 5 rows for Garter st border.

Body Pat
Row 6 (WS): K3, p77.
Row 7: Knit.
Rep Rows 6 and 7 until piece measures approx 16½" from beg; rep Row 6 again—126 total rows including Garter st border. Cut A, leaving a 6" tail to weave in later.

Block 2
First Stripe
Leaving a 6" tail at beg, k across with B.
Row 2 (WS): K3, p77.
Row 3: Knit.
Rep Rows 2 and 3 for 5 times, then rep Row 2 again. Cut B, leaving a 6" tail to weave in later.

Second Stripe
Leaving a 6" tail at beg, k across with C.
Row 2 (WS): K3, p77.
Row 3: Knit.
Rep Rows 2 and 3 for 5 times, then rep

Row 2 again. Cut C, leaving a 6" tail. Alternate First Stripe and Second Stripe for 3 more times.

Last Stripe
Leaving a 6" tail at beg, k across with B. Rep Rows 2 and 3 as for First Stripe for 4 times, then rep Row 2 again.
For Garter st border, k 4 rows. Bind off loosely and kwise.

STRIP 2
Block 3
Beg at the lower edge with B, cast on 80 sts. Knit 5 rows for Garter st border.

Body Pat
Row 6 (WS): P77, k3.
Row 7: Knit.
Rep Body Pat Rows 6 and 7 until piece measures approx 16½" from beg; rep Row 6 again—126 total rows, including Garter st border. Cut B, leaving a 6" tail to weave in later.

Block 4
Leaving a 6" tail at beg, k across with D. Rep Body Pat Rows 6 and 7 as for Block 3 for 60 times, then rep Row 6 again— 122 total rows.
K 4 rows for Garter st border. Bind off loosely and kwise.

finishing
Place strips onto a flat, padded surface. Pin to measurements using rustproof pins. Cover with damp towels, and let dry. Place the 2 strips tog with the RSs out and so the Garter st borders are on all 4 outside edges. Join pieces tog, using a flat seaming method in the center.

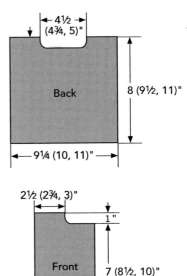

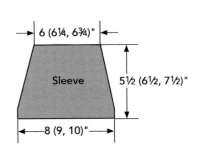

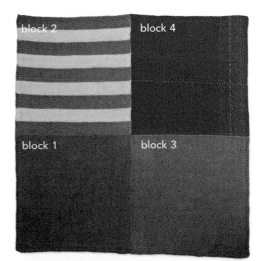

just for
tweens & teens

If you've got a tween or teen in mind for this trio of cool "necessities," check out her favorite colors before you start. The shoulder bag, cell phone case, and cap all sport coordinating stripes and drawstring closures.

DESIGNER: VAL LOVE
PHOTOGRAPHERS: SCOTT LITTLE (*PAGES 52 AND 53*); ANDY LYONS (*OPPOSITE*)

skill level
Easy

finished measurements
Shoulder Bag = 8×10"
Cell Phone Case = 3×7"
Cap circumference = 21" with
    drawstring to adjust fit

yarns
For all three projects:
Patons Grace; 100% mercerized cotton; 136 yds. (122 m); sport weight
● 5 skeins #60705 Cardinal (MC)
● 2 skeins #60134 Royal (A)

needles & extra
● Size 5 (3.75 mm) knitting needles *or size needed to obtain gauge*
● Two double-pointed needles (dpns), size 5 (3.75 mm), for shoulder bag I-cord strap
● Blunt-end yarn needle

gauge
In St st (k 1 row, p 1 row) and using a double strand of yarn, 22 sts and 30 rows = 4" (10 cm).
TAKE TIME TO CHECK YOUR GAUGE.

special abbreviations
Rsl Inc (Right Slant Increase)
Insert left needle from back to front under horizontal "ladder" between two needle points. Knit this lifted strand through the front.
Lsl Inc (Left Slant Increase)
Insert left needle from front to back under horizontal "ladder" between two needle points. Knit this lifted strand through the back.

Notes: Use two strands of yarn together throughout to give the finished pieces a fabriclike quality. The shoulder bag and cell phone case have drawstring closures. Use an I-cord for the bag's shoulder strap. Thread the drawstring around the cap, adjust it, and tie it in a bow to fit.

All three accessories have a fabriclike quality to them because they're knitted with a double strand of yarn in stockinette stitch.

shoulder bag

Using 2 strands of MC and leaving a 36" tail of yarn for finishing, beg at lower edge, cast on 78 sts.
Row 1 (RS): K across.
Row 2: P across.
Row 3: K2, Lsl inc, k36, Rsl inc, k2, Lsl inc, k36, Rsl inc, k2.
Row 4: P82.
Row 5: K3, Lsl inc, k36, Rsl inc, k4, Lsl inc, k36, Rsl inc, k3.
Row 6: P86.
Row 7: K4, Lsl inc, k36, Rsl inc, k6, Lsl inc, k36, Rsl inc, k4.
Row 8: P90.
Row 9: K5, Lsl inc, k36, Rsl inc, k8, Lsl inc, k36, Rsl inc, k5—94 sts.
Work 3 more St st rows, ending with a p row.
Cont in St st, changing color on k rows as follows: 2 rows A, 4 rows MC, 8 rows A, 4 rows MC, 2 rows A.

Change to MC and cont until work measures approx 9½" from base of shoulder bag, ending with a p row.
Next Row (make picot st holes for drawstrings): [K1, (yo, k2tog) across to last st, k1.]
Work 7 St st rows, then rep bet [ ]s to form picot st edging.
Work 5 St st rows.
Leaving a 36" tail of yarn for finishing, thread all sts onto another 36" length of yarn.

finishing

With WSs of bag tog and 1 strand of MC, sew sides tog through both thicknesses, 1 st in from each edge, working from the top to the base. With the same tail, join the base. Fold facing to the inside along the picot edging and, with 1 strand of yarn, hem the stitches (that were saved on the waste yarn) in place above the drawstring holes.
Remove thread as you work. Weave loose ends into the WS of the work. Turn RS out.

I-cord Shoulder Strap: With dpns and a double strand of A, cast on 4 sts and k 1 row.
*Without turning work, push sts to other end of needle.
Next Row: K, pulling yarn tight when working first st**.
Rep from * to ** until strap measures approx 36" from beg; bind off. Weave loose ends into WS of work.
Thread strap through picot hole at side of bag from inside of bag; thread other end through picot hole at opposite side of bag from outside.
Make an overhand knot 1" from each end of strap.

Drawstring Closure (make 2): Cut four 84" lengths of A.
Knot 4 cut ends tog ½" from each end. Loop 1 end over small doorknob. Insert pencil through yarn at other knot; pull tight and twist as much as possible. Remove the pencil.
Fold twisted yarn in half. Remove from door knob. Knot 2 knotted ends tog to prevent unraveling.
Thread other end through picot holes, beg at hole to the right of the left end of shoulder strap.
Going right, weave through the holes to the last hole on opposite side of bag. Knot both ends of drawstring tog 1" from end and trim.
Rep for opposite side with 2nd drawstring.

cell phone case

Using 2 strands of MC and leaving a 30" tail of yarn for finishing, beg at lower edge and cast on 26 sts.
Row 1 (RS): K across.
Row 2: P across.
Row 3: K2, Lsl inc, k10, Rsl inc, k2, Lsl inc, k10, Rsl inc, k2.
Row 4: P30.

Row 5: K3, Lsl inc, k10, Rsl inc, k4, Lsl inc, k10, Rsl inc, k3—34 sts.
Work 3 more St st rows, ending with a p row.
Cont in St st, changing color on k rows as follows: 2 rows A, 4 rows MC, 6 rows A, 4 rows MC, and 2 rows A.
Change to MC and cont until work measures approx 6" from base of case, ending with a p row.
Next Row (make picot st holes for drawstrings): [K1, (yo, k2tog) across to last st, k1.]
Work 5 St st rows, then rep bet [ ]s to form picot edging. Work 3 St st rows. Leaving a 24" tail, thread all sts onto another length of yarn.

finishing

With WSs tog and 1 strand A, sew sides tog through both thicknesses, 1 st in from each edge and working from the top to the base.
With the same tail, join base. Fold facing toward you at the picot edging and using 1 strand of yarn, hem sts (from thread) in place and above drawstring holes. Remove thread as you work. Weave loose ends into WS of work. Turn RS out.

Drawstring Closure: Cut four 36" lengths of MC and follow directions for Drawstring Closure for Shoulder Bag, page 60.

cap

Using 2 strands MC and leaving a 40" tail of yarn for finishing, beg at lower edge and cast on 116 sts.
Row 1 (RS): K across.
Row 2: P across.
Row 3: K8, (Lsl inc, k8) 13 times, ending Lsl inc, k4—130 sts.
Rows 4–6: Work 3 St st rows, beg p.
Row 7 (picot edge): K1, (yo, k2tog) across to last st, k1.
Rows 8–12: Work 5 St st rows, beg with a p row.
Row 13: K8, (k2tog, k7) 13 times, k2tog, k3—116 sts.
Row 14: P across.
Row 15 (drawstring holes): Rep Row 7.
Cont in St st to approx 3" from Row 13, ending with a p row.
Beg stripes on next row as follows: 2 rows A, 4 rows MC, 6 rows A, 4 rows MC, and 2 rows A.

Shape crown—Row 1: K1; (k2tog, k17) 6 times, k1—110 sts.
Rows 2–4: Work 3 St st rows, beg with a p row.
Row 5: K1, (k2tog, k16) 6 times, k1—104 sts.
Row 6: Purl.
Cont as set, evenly dec 6 sts on k rows—56 sts.

Cont evenly dec 6 sts on each row—8 sts.
Cut yarn, leaving a long tail. Thread tail into yarn needle and back through rem 8 sts. Pull up to close opening. Secure in place.

finishing

With RS tog and 1 strand of yarn, sew sides of Cap tog from base to top, 1 st in from each edge.
Fold bottom edge to inside along first picot row and hem just below 2nd picot row for picot border. Weave all loose ends into inside of work.

Drawstring Tie: Cut six 90" lengths A and follow directions for Shoulder Bag drawstrings, page 60.
Thread drawstring through holes around Cap; knot each end 1" from tip and trim. Tie with a bow to adjust fit.

basic pullover

Pair it with jeans or your favorite wool skirt. Add a scarf or a big shawl, cinch a belt around the waist, or leave it plain! Any way you wear it, this pullover is a wardrobe classic.

DESIGNER: ANN. E. SMITH
PHOTOGRAPHER: SILVER LINING

Now that you're comfortable with knitting basics, it's time to work on something that requires a bit of shaping—the kind you'll find on this easy-going number.

sizes

XS (S, M, L, XL, XXL)
Pattern is written for the smallest size with changes for the larger sizes in parentheses. When only one number is given, it applies to all sizes.

Note: *For ease in working, circle all numbers pertaining to the size you're making.*

finished measurements

Chest = 32 (36, 40, 44, 48, 52)"
Length = 22 (22½, 23, 23½, 24, 24½)"

yarn

Lion Brand Homespun (Art. 790); 98% acrylic/2% polyester; 6 oz. (170 g); 185 yds. (167 m); bulky weight
● 3 (4, 4, 5, 5, 5) skeins #336 Barrington

needles & extra

● Size 10 (6 mm) knitting needles *or size needed to obtain gauge*
● Size 8 (5 mm) knitting needles
● Blunt-end yarn needle

gauge

In St st (k 1 row, p 1 row) with larger needles, 14 sts and 20 rows = 4" (10 cm).
TAKE TIME TO CHECK YOUR GAUGE.

instructions

BACK

Beg at the lower edge with smaller needles, cast on 56 (63, 70, 77, 84, 91) sts. K 6 rows for Garter st band. Change to larger needles. Beg with a p row, work in St st (k 1 row, p 1 row) until piece measures approx 15" from beg, ending with a p row. At beg of next 2 rows, bind off 4 sts. Cont in St st on rem 48 (55, 62, 69, 76, 83) sts to approx 21 (21½, 22, 22½, 23, 23½)" from beg, ending with a k row.

Neckband—Row 1 (WS): P11 (14, 17, 20, 23, 26) sts, k26 (27, 28, 29, 30, 31) sts, p to end.
Row 2 and each following RS row: Knit.
Row 3: P10 (13, 16, 19, 22, 25), k28 (29, 30, 31, 32, 33), p to end.
Row 5: P9 (12, 15, 18, 21, 24), k30 (31, 32, 33, 34, 35), p to end. With the RS facing, bind off kwise and loosely.

FRONT

Work as for Back until piece measures approx 19 (19½, 20, 20½, 21, 21½)" from beg, ending with a k row. Work Neckband Rows 1–5.
Shape neck: On next RS row, k13 (16, 19, 22, 25, 28) sts, bind off center 22 (23, 24, 25, 26, 27) sts; k to end.
Right Shoulder: P9 (12, 15, 18, 21, 24), k4. K across next row.
Rep last 2 rows until piece measures approx 22 (22½, 23, 23½, 24, 24½)" from beg, ending with WS row. Bind off kwise and loosely.
Left Shoulder: With WS facing, join yarn at neck edge. K4, p to end. K across next row. Rep last 2 rows to same length as Right Shoulder, ending with WS row. Bind off kwise and loosely.

SLEEVE (make 2)

Beg at lower edge with smaller needles, cast on 31 (32, 34, 35, 37, 38) sts. K 6 rows for border. Change to larger needles and p across next row. Working in St st, inc 1 st (k in front and in back of same st) each edge now. Then inc 1 st each edge every 10th row 3 (2, 0, 0, 0, 0) times, every 8th row 5 (7, 8, 5, 2, 1) times, and every 6th row 0 (0, 2, 6, 10, 12) times. Work even on the 49 (52, 56, 59, 63, 66) sts to approx 18½ (19, 19½, 19½, 19½, 20)" from beg, ending with a p row. Bind off kwise and loosely.

finishing

Join shoulder seams. Set in sleeves, sewing bound-off sts on body to sides of upper sleeves. Join underarm and side seams. Weave in loose ends.

TIP: When you wrap a hand-knit gift, include a label from one of the skeins of yarn you used. That way, the recipient will know laundering instructions.

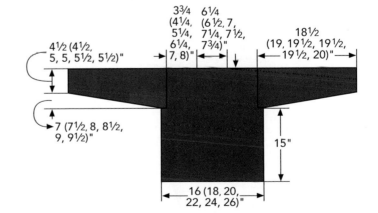

Better Homes and Gardens®
Creative Collection™

Editorial Director
Gayle Goodson Butler

Editor-in-Chief
Beverly Rivers

Executive Editor   Karman Wittry Hotchkiss

Contributing Editorial Manager   Heidi Palkovic

Contributing Design Director   Tracy DeVenney

Contributing Project Editor   Laura Holtorf Collins
Copy Chief   Mary Heaton
Contributing Copy Editor   Pegi Bevins
Proofreader   Joleen Ross
Administrative Assistant   Lori Eggers

Executive Vice President
Bob Mate

Publishing Group President
Jack Griffin

Chairman and CEO   William T. Kerr
President and COO   Stephen M. Lacy

In Memoriam
E. T. Meredith III (1933–2003)
